A Mother's Poem

Helen Millman

Illustrated by Chad Perry

D1444597

Halo
PUBLISHING
INTERNATIONAL

ISBN: 978-1-61244-880-0
Library of Congress Control Number: 2020912404

Printed in the United States of America

Halo Publishing International
8000 W Interstate 10
Suite 600
San Antonio, Texas 78230
www.halopublishing.com
contact@halopublishing.com

This book was inspired by my children: Shai Michael, Guy Ariel and Ben Nathaniel. You are curious, lovable and as fun as can be.

I dedicate this book to you.

You have given me the privilege
of sharing life with you,

4

to laugh, to learn, to whisper;
just how much I love you.

You have given me
the wisdom to trust
my own hat,

to follow your unique
wonder; and to express
despite my doubt.

6

8

You made me chase you, you had me run;
and even carrying you was often fun.

You taught me how a moment
can last a long time,

especially when I enjoy it; and
without noticing myself I hum.

You taught me how to be emotionally naked, without the fear of being exposed.

How to love myself without a proof; that I am better than I was told.

Being smart is often helpful;
yet not as meaningful as kind.

It's hugs and kisses that you wish for;
my giggles, my gentle lullabies.

When I sometimes think about tomorrow;
you remind me how to smile about today.

16

How a rainy day sounds beautiful;
even more so when we play.

You have shown me how strength and courage are not so much alike.

How *powerful* inspires, where
confusion loves to strike.

I hope my child that you remember,
one day when you grow old,

about the beauty that you have
taught me; how it kept my heart
warm despite the outside cold.

Now as my face begins
to age and there is more
that I wish to say,

I thank the angels for granting
me, yet again another day.

Another day with you my love, where discoveries have merely just begun.

24

I will caress your face and your tired cheeks; tonight, I promise not to run.

I promise not to rush or fuss or hurry;
I will listen to your endless tales and dreams.

Your dinosaurs, your jokes, your spellings;
and your once upon a time themes.

CPSIA information can be obtained
at www.ICGtesting.com
Printed in the USA
BVHW050127281020
591756BV00001B/1